A Toast to
St Martirià

Albert Serra
A Toast to St Martirià

Translated from the Catalan by Matthew Tree

With an afterword by Alexander García Düttmann

DIVIDED

Published in the United Kingdom by Divided in 2024.

Divided Publishing
Rue de Manchesterstraat 5
1080 Brussels
Belgium

Divided Publishing
Deborah House
Retreat Place
London E9 6RJ
United Kingdom

https://divided.online

First published in Barcelona in 2023 by H&O Editores as *Un brindis per Sant Martirià*.

Front cover image from Albert Serra's *Singularity* (2015), courtesy Albert Serra
Author portrait © Katharina Huber
Designed by Alex Walker
Printed by Printon, Tallinn

ISBN 978-1-7395161-1-6

This book was translated with the help of a grant from the Institut Ramon Llull.

To all the people from Banyoles who have influenced me, without whom I would not be who I am, especially those who are no longer with us: Ll.C. and F.B.

To all those, be they from Banyoles or not, who have crossed my artistic path and understood what it is I wanted to do.

1

'I started it, I finished it.' —Celso Costa (1928–2009), an entrepreneur from Banyoles.

I don't know if it's appropriate for me to make this speech. I wondered about it when I was asked, and in the end I had to search for some reasons that would make it look appropriate. Two good reasons occurred to me. Right now I'm making a speech for the Banyoles *festa*, and there you have two words: '*festa*' and 'Banyoles'.* Well, I will make a speech that will talk about these two things, because both of these elements – 'Banyoles', '*festa*' – have been very, very important in my life. I'd say that they've been the two most decisive elements in it, and they continue to be so, despite everything, right up to now.

*   Banyoles (population *c.* 20,200), in the province of Girona in north-east Catalonia, is officially a city (Catalan *ciutat*). At once rural and an industrial hub, in English it would be called a town; most of the people who live there, however, call it a village (Catalan *poble*). The Catalan word *festa* (plural *festes*) refers exclusively to partying, whether that be in private houses or in a whole municipality; in the latter case they are called *festes majors*, and are always preceded by a speech, usually given by someone from the town or village in question. The *festa major* of St Martirià, at which Albert Serra delivered the opening speech in 2022, is held in Banyoles in mid-October, and consists of various concerts, a procession of drum-beating people (some of them dressed as dwarfs and giants), displays of human tower-building, a *correfoc* (demons and dragons wielding large fireworks as they cavort through the town), and the dancing of *sardanes* – the Catalan national dance – in which four different *sardana* orchestras compete with each other in the main square. Among other things. —Translator.

I don't think that there is anybody in the contemporary film world — at least at the level at which I find myself in it (that is to say, the level of those people who have been favoured with a certain amount of international recognition as far as the critics are concerned) — for whom playfulness has played such an important role: always, in all my films, right from the start. For me, and I think also for those around me, this has been absolutely fundamental. If things were not done in order to have fun, if there was no trace of *festa* or fraternity in them, they would have been meaningless. To live a humdrum life, a life, let's say, in which there is no element of subversion, presumptuous though that word may sound, is to live a life that may become dull and bereft of interest. This essential concept is linked to and has its origin in a whole group of people from Banyoles who influenced me and who I'd like to talk a little about. I decided to be a film director precisely in order to perpetuate the concepts of *festa* and playfulness. In no way did I want these ideals to be limited to the normal *festa* days celebrated by every village, such as the St Martirià here in Banyoles, or even to birthdays, which are the equivalent of village *festes* on an individual level. Those concepts had to be extended and expanded so that, in fact, they formed part of life, three hundred and sixty-five days a year — which is why, without certain very important collaborations and influences, this agenda could never have been brought to fruition: cinema is an art which is logically based on collective work. When you become aware that life only makes sense if it happens like that, in a natural way, then this ideal almost turns into a political programme, into a programme for life, and if, on top of this, this ideal can be combined with art, and you can go one step further and make it into a way of life or of earning your living, then so much the better.

The concept of 'Banyoles' was very important right from the beginning. Obviously, because I'm from Banyoles, right? Here's a question which I've often asked myself and which is difficult to answer, and you've probably asked yourselves the same thing: would things have been different, would it have been possible to have been what I've been, or to have done what I've done, if I'd come from another place? To what extent has this specific situation, in this specific town, with these specific people, conditioned my life? To what extent have all these factors influenced the fate of a given person? Or, on the contrary, would our individual strength have been enough to have ensured that we developed in a similar fashion, under other influences, in another place? The question of how much leeway, how much power, circumstances have over us, and what percentage of power we have over ourselves, is one of the great dilemmas in life, and, indeed, is always debated in terms of a dialectic between genetics and culture. At which point I'd like to add that I'm always in favour of the importance of culture, which is a choice and therefore a sign of civilisation; and besides, the genetic element is limited to a very specific aspect of personality, which is character, without which, it's true, one can't do anything ambitious, because only character allows us to overcome the fear of failure when we want to set off on previously untrodden paths; and even within the different elements that make up character, one specific part of character is *resolution*. I have never forgotten an extraordinary quote from the Cardinal de Retz, in which he makes the subtlest distinction between *courage* and *resolution*, using a masterful formula: 'Monsieur le comte avait toute la hardiesse de cœur que l'on appelle communément vaillance, au plus haut point qu'un homme la puisse avoir, et il n'avait pas même dans le degré le plus commun, la hardiesse de l'esprit, qui est ce que l'on nomme résolution. La première est ordinaire et même vulgaire; la seconde est même plus rare que l'on ne se le peut imaginer: elle est toutefois encore plus nécessaire que l'autre pour les grandes actions.'* Do not think of this as a paradox; resolution is needed to keep a *festa* going; neither is it a paradox, as I showed in my film *Liberté* (2019), to wish to impose licentiousness by force, using necessary violence.

The concept of 'Banyoles' is, of course, linked to another very important theme. Many of you, certainly those of you who are with me here, have also had to build your professional careers, or have had to live – either for personal reasons, or for any other – in big cities. And here we come across another focus of tension which is both interesting and funny: what are the advantages, what are the drawbacks, of a small town – about the size of Banyoles for instance, which I consider to be pretty much ideal – compared with those of the big city? The magma and the indefiniteness of the big city, above all after the Industrial Revolution, in the eighteenth century, or when the great urban conurbations began to appear a little later on, this

---

*   'The count had all the boldness of heart which we commonly call courage, to the highest extent that any man can, and he did not have, even in the most commonplace degree, the boldness of mind which we name resolution. The first is ordinary, even vulgar; the second is even more rare than we may imagine: it is, however, even more necessary than the other for great deeds.' —Jean François Paul de Gondi, *Mémoires du cardinal de Retz* (1717).

is a theme, a dilemma, a debate, and food for plenty of thought which has both interested and affected many philosophers, many artists, many creators when they wanted to know if they had to move to and earn their living in the big city. And they asked themselves how that would affect their thinking, how it would affect their lives, and, if their thinking was a little more ambitious, how this would affect community life in general when they moved there. There are many theories, but common sense clearly leads us to believe that maybe – as regards the most essential thing in a person's life, their formative years – a small town can be much more beneficial. The heart of the big city is chaotic and its psychological base is the intensification of nervous living, a rapid, uninterrupted succession of external and internal impressions which are difficult for a person, for an individual, to absorb. This can lead to confusion, it can even lead to tedium, simply because of one's inability, well described by Walter Benjamin and Georg Simmel, to assimilate all those sharp, fleeting and intermittent impressions. This tedium happens a lot more frequently than most people think; and despite the fact that it may appear to be another paradox, this tedium is a lot more common in the minds of the inhabitants of big cities than in those of small villages. In theory, big cities have seen the invention of every conceivable form of distraction, precisely in order to mitigate this effect, this tedium; and yet tedium, in an unsettling way, increases. It's a bit like what happens to drug addicts: they give themselves an ever larger dose of a given drug and it has less and less effect. The same thing happens in the city, with the result that this famous tedium, or *spleen*, as they used to call it in the nineteenth century, was born there; the fact is that, so far as creativity is concerned, many

people believe that these are not ideal conditions. To organise all this tedium, to organise all this big city confusion,
something called *reason* was obviously invented, through
the use of which attempts have been made to transform this
tedious confusion into something bearable.

In the big city, most relationships are thus transformed
into more or less intellectual ones, that is to say, based
mainly on personal interests. People are transformed, they
become undifferentiated and are valued only because of
what they contribute. This is not the case in villages, precisely because, since this accumulation of nervous living
does not exist there, there is no need to deal with it: you
don't have to protect yourself from anything, and personal
relationships can be of an emotional kind. I believe this is
the great difference: the contrast between those intellectual relationships based on one's interests, with emotional
ones which are probably based on more irrational, more
essential, more instinctive, more sovereign impulses, and
which mark the way people relate to each other in villages.
And these emotional relationships are not imposed, nor
should they be mythologised. A village is not a family, it
is not a fraternity which is, let's say, absolute, it's not a
given . . . nor does it necessarily *have* to exist. A village is
more or less a community in which people choose to live,
but, as I say, with certain emotions, with relationships that
are manageable and, to some extent, more profound than
those to be found in the cities. I believe that this creates
a certain resilience, because it inevitably puts people's in-
dividuality first: their instincts, their personalities; everything which is excluded in the city is accepted by people
and generates a vital – and I believe an impulsive – way of

living, which is much more intense and, in the long term, if this happens in one's formative years, it generates an even greater resilience.

I've met a lot of people in my life, and the fact is I've hardly ever met anybody – or I could even say I've met absolutely nobody – who was born in a big city and who impressed me; the remarkable people who have crossed my path come from areas which aren't the big city; and it is due to this experience of mine and to my intuition, that I am convinced that all the really strong, resilient people never come from an urban environment or from a big city, where it is much harder to develop a certain firmness of purpose, a certain strength, for the reasons I have just explained.

A city imposes a kind of preciseness, without which it wouldn't function. The same example has been given many times; if the clocks were to remain unsynchronised for just one hour, the resulting chaos would last for days . . . In a village that doesn't happen, you are not under that influence, under the imperative of a life of schematic precision, if I can put it like that. The value of life is to be found precisely – so I think and so everyone who influenced me and who I knew in Banyoles taught me – in singularity, in peculiarity, which are completely alien to any form of plan, and which avoid any kind of uniformity.

As I've said, many philosophers have dealt with this theme, and I read them, not only for the intrinsic debate involved, but also for their usefulness in my own life. In order to take personal decisions about yourself, you can ask for advice, you can think for yourself, or you can go to history's greatest thinkers: even if they're dead we have access to them through their books. Among them there is Nietzsche, for instance; or John Ruskin, the master of Proust, who I've read a great deal of: I read *La Recherche* three times, and although it provides a magnificent portrait of what the city is, or the city at the beginning of the last century, it also provides a magnificent portrait of a life apart, of a solitary life; Georg Simmel, who also influenced me very much and who in some of his books also deals with this theme and all the resultant sociological consequences. (I won't go into a slightly more contemporary theme, how the internet and mobile phones have transformed these theoretical advantages of small towns or villages, have reduced them to almost zero, and we've all ended up living in an uncontrollable, impossible-to-assimilate mental city . . . but that's another subject, and unfortunately now is not the time to talk about it, although I have not been able to resist touching upon it because of the sadness it causes me.)

This, as was inevitable, naturally led all those philosophers to hate big cities and everything they give rise to. This punctilious life, this ordered life, has a god – the god of the monetary economy, which is what regulates the whole thing, and which takes precedence over emotional relationships. And there's also another side of the coin: this god tends to intellectualise existence, and therefore loathes instinctive impulses.

These three elements – the monetary economy, the city in itself as a space full of stimuli, and intellectualism – are used in order to transform and to try and diminish the life force. But of course these three elements face a clear contradiction when they come up against the disturbance represented by local *festes*: that playfulness which I mentioned at the beginning. This playfulness is pure expenditure, as George Bataille would've put it, which does not generate any profit; it is the *accursed share* which is close to being sacred and is not managed by any form of control; on the contrary, it is based on instinct, on a natural fraternity, on impulse, on a desire to satisfy oneself and have a good time which, as you know, is the *joy* so typical of *festes* and is the reason why they are celebrated; and which is also why, in order to prevent them from becoming totally uncontrollable, villages limit them to certain designated days and don't let them go on all year long.

That's what I wanted to disrupt, by which I mean that I wanted to extend it and even to encapsulate it, and now I will explain how. The start of the whole thing is closely linked to the problem to which I've already referred: I lived in Banyoles, but I moved to Barcelona to study at the university, *bypassing*, as Donald Trump would put it, the city of Girona, which at that time also had some universities, I think, I don't remember very well – but at no time did it occur to me or to anyone else I knew, that is to say, more or less respectable people, that one had to study in Girona, instead of which we made a direct bypass, as I had seen people do ever since I was a teenager, when the University of Girona didn't exist as such, and neither was Girona as important or fashionable a city as it is today, although for me it continues to be the same boring, conservative, provincial thing that it always was and always will be, I'm sorry to say. At that time, all the people in Banyoles, mentally, physically, and without hesitation, bypassed Girona and went straight to Barcelona, and all the influences that were here in Banyoles came straight from Barcelona and made us a lot more mentally cosmopolitan when compared to those *other* people who lived, pitifully satisfied, like fattened piglets, in a larger town – Girona – that provided them with all the provincial necessities they required. So this is another concept I'd like to stress: this kind of mental cosmopolitanism – when you don't have anything else – which allows you to adopt all the advantages of a big city without having to take on board any of its defects . . . because it is *mental* and also prevents you from deceiving yourself about the good things in the little place where you live. And that is quite the opposite of the provincialism I have alluded to. And it is possible because when you live here, in Banyoles, as a teenager, people arrive at the weekend bringing all the news from the big city . . . That is to say, news about the world in general. At that time, with that form of mental cosmopolitanism, with the influence of all those people who were older than I was, but still young, influenced by the Barcelona in which they lived and which they abandoned fanatically every weekend (neither did they deceive themselves about the good things in the big city despite having ended up there); inspired by all these people, when I was thirteen, fourteen, fifteen, sixteen years old, I thought that no way would I hang around, and that I'd go straight to Barcelona.

There was this dilemma. This huge dilemma about what would be the use of going to Barcelona and how I could protect myself from this intensification of nervous living which the big city gives rise to. But I did this in a very natural way. I studied Hispanic philology for four years, and then did two years of literary theory and comparative literature, and in between a course in the history of art, which took two more years. All in all, I spent eight years at university. And here is an extraordinary anecdote which illustrates both literally and metaphorically how I protected myself: I don't think there is anybody in the world who has spent eight years in a university without making a single friend or even acquaintance there, albeit in the most superficial way – absolutely nobody, during those eight years. I can safely say that I lived my life there without any kind of human contact with any person whatsoever with the exception of the occasional professor, and even then in such a shallow way that I wouldn't qualify it as contact – of any kind. That's how it was – it was that radical, I'm telling you. Obviously, I wasn't interested. This is something which might seem contradictory, because anyone would say that, in a big city, curiosity would come to the fore – such are the people, the human material (or the *acting material* as Heiner Müller liked to call it, because a big city is a theatre, a permanent spectacle) on offer, such is the fun on offer, that it would seem you simply *have* to be interested in it all.

At the time that didn't strike me as being at all convenient. In fact, I lived a rather curious life. I never went in person to university. *Never* means that I maybe turned up for ten or fifteen per cent of the teaching hours, at most, and maybe not even as much as that; and I never made friends with anyone, never had any acquaintances. As you might imagine, and given what my life has since been, I don't appear to be a shy or unsocial person, quite the contrary: in fact, part of my success is due to my social skills, because once the films are finished, when pure creative energy is no longer needed, a knack or a little propensity for PR comes in very handy. And the slight pleasure which this sociability gives can be perfectly natural, doesn't have to be banal in any way. It can even, absurdly enough, be extremely important at times. Warren Buffett has often told the story of how his life changed when he lost his fear of speaking in public (thanks to the courses of Dale Carnegie, which he attended; I read his books . . . when, in fact, I didn't need to, even though you always get something out of them). Warren Buffett even claims that much of his success began that very day. So in this sphere I also have a certain responsibility – a shared one in this case; I believe that we (when I say *we* I mean myself, Montse Triola and all the people who formed Andergraun Films), precisely because we shared this past based on instinctive human relationships, not on intellectual ones, were able to express ourselves in the world of PR, which is usually understood to be a world full of falseness and self-interest, almost comparable to merchandising, to selling products; well, all of us have been able to express ourselves in a far more natural manner, surprisingly so in comparison with that of everyone else in that world, and this has been one of the keys to our success. But as I said, this has been the result of a natural evolution: I had the germ of sociability inside me, and I am, as I say, quite a social person. Nonetheless, at university I didn't want – and that is exactly the right word – I didn't *want* to meet anybody at all.

There is also another miraculous thing that happened during my time at university. For many people it would

seem that the outcome of a life is the fruit of a whole series
of orderly, linked elements, but the truth is quite the opposite; and I like to think that in the film world this is even
more exaggerated, and that I have learnt to adapt myself
to it extremely well. A very funny anecdote from the years
I spent at university, aside from not having met a single
soul, is as follows: to finish all my courses I only needed
one more subject, a difficult subject called Spanish syntax
II or Spanish syntax III, I can't remember which; it was a
very difficult and very technical subject, and I had no intention of studying it and nor did I wish to, although I always
thought that if I could do so properly it would be a sign of
intelligence, because language creates and expresses logi-
cal thinking; but, in the end, I was in my own world at the
time, following my routine of never visiting the university
building nor listening to anything that went on there . . .
The day of the exam arrived and at the last moment I simply couldn't face going in (I hadn't spent even a single day
in class); I hated the whole business, something which is
incomprehensible because I considered that I had a gift
for this subject, and, finally, I decided not to do this exam,
which would have made things extremely complicated for
me because it was the last subject, and I would've had to go
back to university six months or a year later (at that time, if
I'm not mistaken, they were already thinking about making
it possible to re-sit exams in September). That would have
been an absurd complication, but it was such a huge bore
to have to study that subject that I decided not to.

In spite of this, at the last moment, on the very day of the
exam, without having studied, due to an esoteric impulse
or because of some kind of providential human intuition

(intuition being a quality which is rendered impotent by big city life where it is faced with the rigid, schematic precision of events, but which in small towns or in the country is a useful guide, because there life is governed by impulses), due to a sudden physical tension, a final intuitive blow, I got out of bed and, after much doubt, went over to the university, arriving fifteen or twenty minutes late for the exam. There, outside the open door, I saw a large crowd of people and a kind of commotion going on inside the classroom, sheer chaos, people coming out into the cloister, on the ground floor of the Central University of Barcelona, into Plaça de la Universitat, back into the old building, and I thought: 'I've made a mistake, it can't be this classroom.' I went to another classroom, looked around for a while, then checked the notice board, and asked people; time was getting on, time that turned out to be providential for me . . . In the end I understood that it looked as if the classroom really was where I'd thought it was, so I went over and asked what was going on, and a student told me: 'The professor hasn't turned up.' Then I saw a person come out with a list of names, and again I heard people say, 'The professor hasn't turned up and they've made a list of people's names, they've made a note of people's names,' and I saw that the person with the list was at the threshold of the door, about to emerge – I was outside – and I stared at his piece of paper with the names on it, like an alcoholic in front of a bottle, and, alarmed, I said to him: 'Hey, hey, hey, hey, hey . . . Me, me, me!' I barred his way and took the list from him: 'Did you write my name down?' He said to me: 'You . . . Where were you? But you're here outside . . . Who are you, what are you doing out here?' And I answered: 'No man, no, I was inside, I only came outside for a moment, there was a long queue inside of people waiting for their names to be put down and I got distracted, and what was it you wanted . . . ?' And when he heard these last few mysterious words, he replied: 'Ah, OK . . . OK, OK . . .' And he put me down on the list. All the students passed the exam because the professor hadn't turned up; because people were on that list, well, they let them pass the exam. And so I got my degree in Hispanic philology, something which would probably never have happened without that last, apparently useless effort to get out of bed and get over to the university; and my life would have changed, and I don't know if I would be standing before you now as an illustrious and exemplary citizen.

Since that day I got into the habit, during film shoots, which started much later, of always shooting a little more at the end of the day, and then a little bit more, until nothing more could be done because we were just too exhausted. In fact, at university I never understood why most students didn't study right up until the last moment, before being obliged to close their books just seconds before an exam, as that is the moment when you're physically closest to the writing and, logically enough, it is easier to remember the things you've just memorised. That experience also taught me, for good, that the beginning of a day's shoot is a convention, but that the end depends on an unknown logic which cannot be predicted, and thus there should be no timetables or work-time restrictions at that time, for the good of what is being created. To what extent, as I said, would changing those village-based influences, changing the people who influenced me, have led me to a similar destiny? Right now that's quite difficult for me to think and to believe; though it is true that, in this tension between individual impulse and collective context, in the artist in-dividual impulse tends to prevail — so perhaps I would've arrived at the same point — but by different paths.

But what exactly was I doing in Barcelona? Well, I was seeing the same people as I saw here in Banyoles. The same people I saw here at weekends, I also saw in Barcelona from Monday to Friday. And I didn't know that many peo-ple outside this Banyoles group, really; I lived the same life in Barcelona as I did in Banyoles, and it strikes me as a curious thing that after all those years I never made any new friends; I don't know of a similar case to mine. I always think that this is the source of my strength. And, in fact, everything has stayed much the same: that is to say, I still talk almost always, not necessarily with the same people, because some of them have changed, but with a very few people, and almost never with new people (ex-cept for those who have come into my life for subsequent professional reasons, something which of course happened much later). This is another element which I think is im-portant. Aside from the professional side of life, which we all have to deal with, the rest of my life consists in always talking with two or three or four other people. There is absolutely nobody else, I have no interest in going to any kind of event, nor in meeting anyone else at all. That's the way things are, and from the very beginning I realised that it was the only way to protect myself from the incessant stimulation of the city. And right up the present day, I can say that when I'm here in Banyoles I follow the same routine, go to the same restaurants; I always come back to Banyoles, if I can, at weekends, and I usually take an interest in the same things as always.

It's the importance of the frame, as Georg Simmel pointed out – he wrote a very nice essay in which he talked of how frames – picture frames – influenced somewhat the way in which we look at a picture; I once gave a talk in which I extrapolated that idea into the spiritual realm, especially with regard to helping the creative act, and I made it clear that everything important has to fit in a frame and that that frame has to be closed and compact – like that of a painting, which keeps everything enclosed within it – so as to better reflect and contrast what's inside, without making it vibrate. That's the kind of frame which counts. If this closed conceptual frame – as I've been able to see for myself later, after so many films, and above all after the initial preparations for so many films – contains certain essential elements which function and harmonise with each other right from the start, then the film can't go wrong, it can't be bad, just as there can never be a failed life. The frame is the guarantee of that.

I have tried to keep this frame strong and intact for a very long time, and mine was an extremely restrictive frame. Nonetheless, and here is where another stage of my life begins, as would become clear later on, there was a moment when there was a sense of anguish, a seed, which became manifest in a latent impulse to break the frame, but only in one particular direction: that of internationalisation, of thinking about moving abroad, about worldwide glory,

synonymous with that mental cosmopolitanism that I mentioned to you before; the anguish of feeling that, despite
the unequivocal reality of the whole physical world, the
very world in which I was developing, that world was not
especially important; and even though where I physically
found myself was a place that was inevitable, there was another world beyond, an unknown international world, the
world of the elite. It was a kind of abstraction at that time,
in my own mind, a mind which identified with things I'd
read in the papers: with an unreal world, which wasn't exactly passing close by me, because many of the things that
interested me at that time didn't happen even in Barcelona
or in Madrid: they were happening in New York, in Paris,
in London, and they were happening to people, that is to
say artists, to people I wished to emulate, and all that gave
me a sensation, a fairly strong desire for internationalisation: an abstract one, but one which was real enough, and
which little by little came to take possession of me.

Something similar is expressed in that famous sentence
that goes: 'If you don't like the news that you read in the
papers, make some news yourself; do something powerful
or unusual and you'll end up in the papers yourself, and
maybe you'll like what you read, the news will interest you
again.' This theory influenced me a lot during that period, but the concept of internationalisation was abstract, it
wasn't even tied up with success or anything like that, but
rather had to do with artists who were in the world, meaning in other worlds, and when you read about or learnt
something about them, or about their work, which was of
course a primary obsession, those names were always connected with major cities, because news is always generated

in a major city: when a book is published, when a film is premiered, when there's a major film festival . . .

I obviously had no wish to travel – just as I had no wish to meet anybody or to visit anything, no wish to leave this extremely restrictive frame within which I lived. In fact, and this is something else which is quite surprising, I got on my first plane when I was twenty-four – and I might well have waited another six years, until an actor who is present here finally took *his* first plane, in 2006, to go to an unedifying thing which was, and still is, called the Málaga Film Festival. (But, although I would've liked to have waited until then, I can't honestly say that by then that would have been my first plane: I had already been on three.) I took my first plane, to Italy, when I was at university and doing my history of art course.

One possibility was to go by bus, but as I was from Banyoles I was fed up with taking buses; and there was the possibility of taking the plane, to get there quicker. 'Oof, a bus . . . a long time stuck inside that thing, with a lot of people . . .' Forty or fifty people took the bus. On the plane, apart from the professors, there were three other students. At the age of twenty-four, I had never been on a plane, I didn't really know what an aeroplane was; well, for that matter, my grandmother didn't even see an escalator until she was eighty, and she got on her first plane when she was eighty-seven . . . to go to New York with me, just the two of us! We just weren't interested in planes. I made up for this later and have now become an aeronautics expert, partly thanks to books, above all Wolfgang Langewiesche's classic *Stick and Rudder*, but also, obviously, thanks to the countless flights I have taken all over the world: I must be one of the people of my age who has flown the most. After Italy I made my first trip to New York, also paid for out of my own pocket, because I was so impressed by that city . . . One day, in that period, I walked past a travel agency on Barcelona's Gran Via, before the fall of the Twin Towers. There was an offer in the window and I went in and bought it. And I went to New York. Since then I have paid once or twice to go back to New York, and two or three times to visit Italian cities. Never again in my life have I paid to go anywhere else, nor has travel ever interested me, nor have I wanted to visit any particular place, or to find out anything from anyone who wasn't one of the people I already knew; and, in fact, often when I went to these cities, I didn't know what I was looking for, because my life there took its course in exactly the same way as it did in Barcelona; that is to say, I didn't do much at all, didn't go to many museums, didn't do much of anything. I simply tried to protect myself from that nervous city living and, by contrast, I often struggle in vain to establish some kind of emotional link with all that; that is to say, and this is something I can in all modesty recommend to you if you were born in a good place, a small town such as Banyoles: you can save yourself the trouble, don't do it, you don't have to go anywhere because the experience you'll get out of it isn't worth the effort or the lost time or the wasted money (and nowadays it's difficult to get hold of any). These cities are machines to destroy, not create – or, as Michel Houellebecq says, machines to destroy love. None of my idols has ever recommended moving away from home. This attitude is quite the contrary of that myth perpetrated by foolish wealthy people who send their children off to study abroad so that they can see the world and learn . . . And let's not even talk about those people who visit cities with small children and all the psychological chaos that it causes; it's funny to think that maybe in this case it's the city which, suddenly defenceless despite all its powerful machinery, now has to protect itself from invasion . . . In fact, in one of John Waters's famous sayings – he's always coming up with famous sayings – in one of his most recent, he says: 'Take it easy, you don't need to pay an impossibly high rent in one of the big cities, nothing interesting is happening in New York, London, Paris, Berlin . . . that you don't already know about.' He means: 'I've been there and I'm telling you: there's nothing interesting there that you don't already know.'

Karl Lagerfeld also said that throughout his entire life he'd never travelled anywhere. Only for work. Another of my idols, who sadly died recently, he had one of the largest private book collections in the whole of Europe (not bibliophile books for collectors, but modern books whose contents you could use); some people said there were three hundred thousand. I spoke to his bookseller who told me: 'No, that's a lie, there weren't three hundred thousand, he'd managed to get to a million.' If anybody has the tiniest idea of what that quantity means – maybe Jona Solana does, who is here today – of what *exactly* a million, or three hundred thousand, books means . . . If it was even three hundred thousand it made him one of the biggest collectors in Europe, or *the* biggest – and if he had a million . . . I wrote once about my relationship with books . . . Michael O'Leary, the CEO of Ryanair and another of my idols (I must be the only person in the world who has six different books about him at home) said in an interview: 'I don't give a shit if no one likes me. I'm not a cloud bunny or an aerosexual. I don't like aeroplanes. I never wanted to be a pilot like those other platoons of goons who populate the airline industry.' He only travels once a year, when he goes on holiday. Which is something quite unusual for someone who's the head of an airline that's always been known for its progressive innovation, and which has ended up being the company which carries more passengers than any other in Europe, a lot more than Lufthansa or Air France or British Airways, all those huge companies that everyone sees everywhere. Given that he had no interest in the subject, it would seem that for him the whole business of travel and aeroplanes has proven very fruitful. As you can imagine, I was never interested in cinema and now you can begin to understand why.

But these are the kind of people who, as I say, also have their frame, their mental frame, which somehow makes its contents shine. And this frame, which closes itself off so that nothing can get in, and so that nothing can escape, protects them. Only this can explain why, after having insulted transport ministers, prime ministers, the heads of other airline companies, the most important regulatory bodies of the European Union, the European Union in general (and all this in one of the most regulated markets in the world!), O'Leary ended up creating the airline that carries more passengers than any other in the world, an airline which has had the least accidents – in fact, no accidents at all! – (and there is no need for me to remind you here of the Germanwings – which is to say, Lufthansa – accident in which several people from Banyoles died, who we all know; nor do I need to remind you of the Air France accident which took place in the middle of the Atlantic a few years ago); in short, O'Leary created the most efficient airline of them all. I won't talk here about his mentor, Herb Kelleher, who influenced me with regard to filmmaking in two ways, which I don't have time to explain fully here and can only briefly mention: concern yourself only with the crew, and not with the viewer (Kelleher was only concerned with his workers, and not his customers); and take a free-and-easy view of day-to-day business (a film producer is a private company, with all that being a company entails).

I only took two trips at that time, and there's a coincidence that's so extraordinary (some people know about it, and I've talked about it more than once) that I never tire of repeating it, or, rather, of repeating myself. Both of these trips began in Banyoles, on the mornings of two separate days. The first involved Senyor Ramon Masgrau, Senyor Josep Ollé and myself; we were in a bar reading the paper, and someone said, 'The Cannes Film Festival is on.' I don't remember what year it was, maybe ninety-six or ninety-seven. 'Have you seen this? The Cannes Festival is on.' And I said, 'Why don't we go?' And that afternoon we'd already got to Cannes, by car – without internet or anything, obviously. We spent three days there, in the most spontaneous and natural way, just the way I'm telling it. Obviously, we didn't know anything, we didn't know that at Cannes you can only see films if you've got accreditation: without accreditation you can't see anything official. So when we were there, the only thing we could do during those three days was walk up and down the seafront; or along the port with its huge luxury yachts, which we liked because we could see the owners having lunch and dinner on board; or through the central streets, in front of the red carpet-covered stairs: and then we went to have lunch, and dinner, then walk, then sleep, then walk again, one thing after the other, and the next day was the same. You can probably sense right now that these movements might be a metaphor – or a simile – which is quite perfect for those journeys which I have never taken and which nobody ought to take because in the end this is what they end up turning into.

But, and this is the other extraordinary coincidence, another day, the day of the second trip, in the morning I read the following in the paper: 'Atom Egoyan presents the film *Exotica* at the Locarno Festival.' And I said to myself: 'Locarno . . . why don't I go?' And, all alone, on this occasion, I immediately took a train to Girona, then caught the train to Milan where I caught a night train which left that evening – and by midday I was in Locarno. In the end I was able to talk briefly with Mr Egoyan, shake his hand for a moment before the showing on the impressive Piazza Grande. And two days later I went home. Atom Egoyan, a Canadian of Armenian origin, is a person I've since met frequently in many different places, and we always have lively conversations; his wife is also a fantastic person. We even gave a masterclass together in the form of a dialogue at the Toronto Festival; of course he doesn't remember that first brief meeting because I was a nobody, but I do. He is quite an interesting person, although his latest films, unfortunately, are less so – they're getting worse and worse; as a person however, he has remained, let's say, very likeable, just the way I saw him that day . . . I only shook his hand briefly, but he has remained just as he was then. But what an extraordinary coincidence:

there are film festivals all over the world (and this says much in favour of the frame I mentioned and of always keeping it very restricted and of not allowing anything to leave it unless it really is because instinct or impulse, without one knowing why, demands it) – what an extraordinary coincidence, I could have gone to a thousand film festivals around the world, to San Sebastián, to Berlin, to Venice, there are thousands of them everywhere, so what an incredible coincidence that the only two film festivals that I visited, when I was just over twenty, and wanted to be a writer and not a film director, happened to be Cannes and Locarno. Life has gone by, I have made six feature films, five of them have been presented at the Cannes Festival – the latest in the Official Selection, up for the Palme d'Or – and the only one which wasn't presented at Cannes won the Golden Leopard at Locarno! All of my films have been premiered at these two festivals. And if that isn't an extraordinary coincidence, then please forgive me for saying it is. There must be an esoteric explanation, or a rational one, I don't know, but for me, even now, it is completely inexplicable. One possibility, which would lie halfway between the two explanatory options, and which has become emblematic for me, is the reply which the millionaire Charlie Munger gave one day when they asked him – when he was almost ninety – what he thought, he being a man of great experience, was the key to success in life. And he answered: 'From a strictly practical point of view, after all these years, I've discovered that the most important factor for achieving success is, above all, to deserve it.' And then he went into all kinds of mathematical details and said that if you deserved it, you had an eighty-five per cent greater chance of achieving success.

I also remember that, coming back from my trip to Locarno, I took the same Milan train, also a night train, which reached Girona at five or six in the morning; I remember that it was a Sunday, and I hitch-hiked to Banyoles from Girona, like I always used to do, and an impressive car stopped, a huge one, a BMW 7 Series, if I'm not mistaken. It was already light, and when I sat down, the driver politely shook my hand and said 'I'm' – what was his first name? I don't remember – 'Manxa.' And I said, 'Manxa, of the Can Manxa hardware store?' 'Yes, I'm the boss of Can Manxa.' He was the owner – maybe he still is, I imagine he's alive, I don't know, he was middle-aged twenty-five years ago – of the famous Manxa hardware store in Olot, not the one in Banyoles. He told me: 'I'm Manxa, of Can Manxa, I'm from Olot.' And he dropped me off at my door when I came back that day from Locarno.

Clearly, all this took place within a well-structured frame. And now, if we don't want to go on too long, it's time to really take a look at what was inside this frame. I think I've made it fairly clear what the frame's about. What there was inside this frame, as you can well imagine, and as I wrote in the dedication I included at the beginning of this book, are the people who influenced me, all those people from Banyoles who made the films possible and allowed them to be made in the very special way I mentioned at the beginning, in which playfulness was always the first and most important thing, and I think that right up until now this has remained the case, identical to the

way it was at the start of everything, doing honour to everything which never changes, even though the world has
indeed changed for the worse . . . But the complications
involved in making the films hasn't changed; in fact the
way of shooting them, of making them, is fairly similar
to the method I have always used; however, it's also true
that over time it's been necessary to overcome a stronger
resistance than existed before, and to impose playfulness,
as if it were a political programme; and the outside people, by which I mean the international co-producers, have
had to be made to understand that this playfulness is
an essential element and that it cannot be allowed to be
lost, and that without it nothing would be done, and that
would be that.

As I've said, the people who influenced me, and who were
a lot more important even than myself with regard to this
vision, were *people*: real people. Because, in the end, a town,
especially a small town, in which these distinctions can still
be made, is made up of people, of citizens, as some – not
me – prefer to call them, of individuals, some of them singular ones. Obviously there have to be some public repre-
sentatives who organise everything; obviously there have to
be some public facilities; obviously everyone would prefer
that things work rather than that they don't; and obviously,
it is inevitable that there is a certain type of social cohesion
based on institutions; personally, and speaking as an artist,
none of this is of any use to me whatsoever and, as you can
imagine, if the university was of no use to me, no form of
village social organisation has helped me in any way; on the
contrary, it was more of an inconvenience, it was a nuisance,
because all the forms of relationship with the people who

influenced me – and this is another constant factor to be found in all my films – began in and were based on a playful atmosphere. And playful atmospheres, despite everything, are connected to the night, and it is there where all the values and that emotional dimension which I told you about right at the beginning, that sovereign impulse behind the kind of relationships which can exist in villages, all this loses its balance, and the night can intensify this even further and can make it more original.

This is a subject which is a little complicated to explain because it has a lot of nuances, it can lead to misunderstandings, and it involves a lot of people. It starts with an idea which is also very basic, which we could talk about for hours, and which is very Catalan, very much part of the early twentieth-century avant-garde, a little Spanish too, at any rate very Mediterranean, very southern European, and this is the concept of the *tertúlia*,* which is something that existed until recently; in fact, Dalí always explained that when Picasso went to Paris, after living in Barcelona, he was sad because he missed the *tertúlies*. What I mean is that such forms of fraternity are disappearing. All the people who began to influence me came from there, from those conversations, conversations which went on into the small hours. As you know, people, even apparently conservative people, become transformed at night, and the ambivalence of their comments, the ambivalence of their personalities, increases; suddenly, they can come out with coarse opinions, a hidden

---

*   A *tertulia* is a regular but informal meeting of usually likeminded people (writers, artists, etc.) who talk about everything under the sun, with no fixed agenda. *Tertúlies* usually take place in cafés and bars.
—Translator.

facet of their personalities, or maybe an insight into their
intimate lives which is not exactly what is seen in public, in
daylight. Once there was enough trust, this new world un-
furled itself before my astonished eyes, and that was a very
important element, I think, because that kind of fraternity
can only be generated by means of trust and respect; in
these beginnings, in these initial moments, in which there
was no other interest than the wish to share. (Because afterwards, I would transform it in the films, and everything
would be based on trust, on that particular form of intimacy, but with a lack of respect: because in the films, for
a whole series of circumstances which I won't go into here
and which I have explained in many talks, lack of respect is
an essential element, that generates forms of vulnerability
which in the end evoke certain forms of innocence and so
on; that aside, in the films there is a hidden interest which
corrodes trust: the selfish interest in making an aesthetic
work of art.) It was taking part in all those early *tertúlies*, as
I was saying, which made me discover the playful element
– everything was thinkable, everything was possible – and
which also made me discover the concept of the night in
a broad, almost spiritual, sense. All the films that I have
made come under the nocturnal psychological umbrella,
but I have made two or three which also have the night
as a specific theme, and in particular this unbalancing, or
transmutation, of those values which appear at night; and
those first *tertúlies* were fundamental in understanding this,
in realising what it meant, and, above all, as I said at the
beginning, in wanting to perpetuate it over time, which is
the most difficult part – and in my case, thanks to my cinematographic praxis, to some extent, I have managed to do
just that, despite all the difficulties involved.

I can't mention all the people who inspired me because the list would be endless and wouldn't be of much interest; it's of interest to me and nobody else, so I won't bore you with the details or the names of these people. By way of a tribute, maybe I could mention, for example, the tennis *tertúlies* (Francesc Bravo, Ramon Masgrau); and another type of person (Jordi Pau); or younger people I didn't know and who oddly enough were also from Banyoles (Jimmy Gimferrer, Montse Triola, Àngel Martín). All these people, in some way, these starting points, this whole drive towards emotional relationships, took place mainly at night. Including very conservative people, like Francesc Bravo, who was a considerable influence and explained certain things that he didn't tell anybody else and precisely because of the heterogeneous nature of this friendly, trustful relationship which didn't exist in any other context, nor could exist in any other except for that one, to the extent that many of our conversations, about incredible things he knew about (and, to be quite clear, I'm not going to repeat any of them here because I'm still afraid it might be illegal to do so), were truly extraordinary.

By way of an example, as regards the legal side of things, also linked to the night although for a different reason (the darkest side of the night), at the age of five I'd heard the word 'methadone' several times, and I continued to hear it over many years; later I forgot about it, but when I had to shoot a film with a particular person, this word and everything it implied, even as far as behaviour was concerned, held no secrets for me. That was something I also learnt about in Banyoles. That nocturnal life, in the good sense of the word, of course, also made me see that there existed a latent life, probably more genuine and more profound than the life which unfortunately most of us have to live, worn out by routine, worn out by everyday life, and so on.

What means do we have at hand to prevent ourselves from being totally worn out? *Festes*. That intermediate movement which breaks up routine, which breaks up everyday life, which breaks our dulled perception of reality, our fatigued senses, and opens up another world which is untouched and unpredictable. On top of which, if you take this aspect of the night, and you add the spirit of playfulness, which is already incorporated into it − and which mutually influence each other − and you add another element, which is the purely artistic one, that is to say, the creation of a work of art, I believe that this is when we finally manage to square the circle. At a given moment I asked myself, 'Why don't we seal all this up?' It seemed to me it was the only way to make it work; that is to say, the only way to ensure that our everyday life did not become permanently worn out. *Festes*, from time to time, are not enough, despite everything, to make their mark or put a brake on the wearing out of our habits. If we want them to continue, what tool, what element can help us to do so? And it occurred to me − clearly influenced by all the people I've told you about, and driven by an urgent, personal need (we are talking about the early 2000s) − that there was something new that could turn things upside down and make possible that squaring of the circle; I am referring to digital technology, which provided easy access to all the technology involved in the field of cameras, home computers, editing programs, and so on, and that you could do yourself. With a bit of help, obviously. In this case, the inestimable help of Xavier

Pérez, who you all know, was extremely important — we spent hour after endless hour working with this precarious technology, but which, at the same time, in that context, made it possible for the frame to close and at the same time to open itself up to the artistic form.

This was, obviously, a revelation, for a reason which I will try to explain in the text below, which was an impromptu presentation which I did in Barcelona for the screening of *Honor de cavalleria* (*Honour of the Knights*, 2006), at the Filmoteca de Catalunya, as a homage to Lluís Carbó, a few years after his death.

The film *Honor de cavalleria* is important above all for several rather random reasons. At the time, it represented something innovative linked to the appearance of digital technology, which for me and for other filmmakers could be used to do anything: that is to say, one could have exactly the same ambitions as when making 35mm films. This ambition could even lead you, in my own case, to make an adaptation of *Don Quixote*, which didn't seem to be something very suitable, given that back then, at the start of the digital era, it wasn't normal to use this technology for that kind of project; it was more habitually associated with things which were urban, contemporary, young. So to think that this technology could also be used to adapt a great literary classic in a fairly loose way — while being faithful to it in spirit — was, frankly, something new. This film partook of this wish to use digital technology for something different, a proposal which, as I've said, was both important and innovative.

That aside, it is clear that today we need to talk about the influence of Lluís Carbó. I think that you can easily judge his work as an actor yourselves, not just in the film we're going to see today, but in all the ones which he made with me later on. But perhaps now is the moment to highlight and specify exactly what his influence was, what the decisive role he played with regard to the production of the films was, and also on a personal level – a big subject – but above all with regard to the films, in which I believe his influence left a deep mark on the whole practice, the whole methodology, which he defined for evermore.

I'd known him since forever, my whole life, we might say, more or less superficially, more or less profoundly, and I got to know him better thanks to an amateur film which we did together called *Crespià*, shot in 2000. This was the first moment, a little bit by chance, that I asked him if he wanted to act. I only wanted to work, of course, with non-professional actors. And from the moment we edited that first film, I realised that he had the gift of being photogenic, in the broadest sense of the word. That is to say, as you know, that there are people who you film and you just can't stop looking at them because everything they do is interesting, and then there are people who are completely the opposite: they might be very good actors, but they're boring.

They don't have that gift of being photogenic in a borderline sense, plastic and spiritual at the same time. At the beginning, this surprised me a little, especially when

I compared him with all the other actors in the film, who didn't have anything like his magnetic attraction – in fact, none of them even came close; on the other hand, he stood out in a very clear way in a primitive, photogenic sense.

From then on in this film, but also a little beforehand, he brought with him an element which was already in my spirit in a quite natural way, but which he consolidated in a much stronger fashion – *playfulness*: because of his character, his inclination, his unpredictable remarks, and especially because of his mental independence with regards to many aspects of life, which was marked by moments of a certain eccentricity, some of which even eventually led to extremes that were almost grotesque (although he had what we might call a relatively normal life). But, in some way, his extravagant moments, and those which were less so, defined a personality which was based on playfulness as a basic axis of the reality of being alive and being with people.

This, I realised, merged technically with digital technology in the most perfect manner, and if I decided to be a film director it was precisely because digital technology made it possible, or easier, to work on the idea of making films in a completely playful, funny way, and that was what drove me towards this particular artistic discipline: the possibility of being able to live a genuinely different life. Seeing that, over the years, life was becoming something ever more boring, repetitive and monotonous, I thought that by making films in this way I could even change my own life and, by extension, that of the people around me. Lluís Carbó's influence, in this sense, was to really show, in an involuntary way, that this was feasible, and, at the very first moment, at the start of making a film, when this idea was very much to the fore, playfulness gave meaning to everything we were doing and gave meaning to most of the risks we were taking, to the very ambition of doing something, because ambition without this playfulness is something dry, a little sterile: formal ambition for its own sake. On the other hand, when accompanied by playfulness, it took on a much more interesting resonance; it became much jollier and kept boredom at a distance for good, and at the same time enriched the film in quite a special way which put vigour and savageness into the work of the actors thanks to this artificial, deliberately provoked and essential thing which is playfulness, and which together with everything else defines the singular tone of all the films I made with him.

Obviously this developed in a way that was increasingly complex, until we get to what is perhaps the definitive masterpiece, even for him, and which I made for the Venice Biennale: *Singularity* (2015). In this film there are countless unforgettable scenes and extremely long moments, minute after minute after minute of pleasure with his sophisticated presence, combined with that of some other actors, most of whom wouldn't even exist without him, because it should be said that, in any given scene, anything that the other actors did always lagged behind what he did.

He could really pull you up, motivate you, not in a superficial way, but by throwing out a whole series of unpredictable vectors which had their consequences and which at the same time improved the reactions of the others due to the very originality of the vectors which he spread around, threw out in a somewhat unconscious way. This had a profound driving effect on a scene and generated a tremendous richness. If not, things would've been much flatter. The risk with many minimalist films is precisely that they are too flat, but, thanks to him, our film avoided that danger and became something which had that singular tone which ends up defining all my films, especially *Singularity*, where it is taken to an extreme which is very, very radical, and, from my point of view, highly original – and, when it comes down to it, brilliant.

Something else which is quite interesting is that he – without being a highly educated person, without being a person the least bit involved in the cultural world – immediately understood the importance of the final result. He understood that this result was transcendent, and not because it might win applause at film festivals – something which in general also gives people a certain sense of security when they're wondering if what they've done has any value. Quite independently of that, he immediately realised the value of the final *aesthetic* result, in which the traces of his personality were nuanced, though on the screen they were, apparently, a little attenuated in comparison with who he was in real life. Despite this, he was well aware that this result was superior, even, to the typical behaviour or the typical attitude which he would have naturally, in real life. And that's something which not many people are able to do: simply being aware – without being highly educated, without understanding all the formal logic that is hidden behind a film – of this improvement. But he, despite everything, with his intuition alone, quite profound I would say, was aware of this value. And from the moment he became aware of it, which was during the shooting of that first film, he always concentrated faithfully on and submitted to that ulterior objective. He always understood that all the things that were not asked of him, or that I found excessive, had their place outside the shoot, but not in the shoot itself – but this didn't prevent him from developing them during the shoot in a different way, a quite repetitive one in many cases, and yet also in a much more precise one. And this final precision of his deserves to be recognised. It's rather a surprising thing, I think, for someone who isn't educated, someone who had no background in culture or cinema, to be able to understand this.

Obviously, that had consequences in real life which were linked indirectly to the films. A film is not only a shoot, but also involves countless sessions of post-production, which we did in Banyoles, and which he attended almost every day; there were also the countless, completely preposterous, trips, about some of which alone a whole book could be written – like the two times we went to Mar del Plata in Argentina, with six or seven people, which was by a long chalk the most insane thing I have ever seen. But he was always aware of that basic idea, he never forgot about it. He knew that on occasion, at some of the screenings, I'd make a joke: 'I have lived countless unsettling moments of total madness, which have been so fun and original that most people couldn't even imagine them, let alone live them . . . But on the other hand I have never seen these actors be as sublime as they are here on screen.' Somehow he knew how to absorb all this influence: the best of himself, the best of me, the best of all the people who were close to this production, in which everybody came to strip themselves of all their egotism and their wish to be a star and find this ulterior good which is the magic and fascination that can only be found when people really know how to be in their exact right place and at the same time never cease to be themselves, with all their potential, all their exhibitionism and all their naturalness.

His innocence also remained with him through to the end, even though we made a great many films, and I'd like it if people could compare that with this last film that I mentioned, *Singularity*, which is a little difficult because it's a thirteen-hour installation which has to be shown in museums. But it's a narrative film full of dialogue which, to a certain extent, confirms his aforementioned innocence. You can clearly see the evolution of this precision, of this ultimate concentration and of this almost ethereal delivery. He was really tired, was undergoing chemotherapy and so on. However, somehow, the filming revived his body. I recall with emotion the last shoot in Ireland. When we got there he could hardly walk, but, after having spent ten or twelve days in the cold and rain, drinking alcohol and doing, in other words, more or less the things he wasn't allowed to do in real life, or which the doctors didn't think were acceptable – not that he was particularly excessive . . . but, well, he did enough – he came back completely transformed – I mean he was walking perfectly well, he was almost running. This is what made his acting so subversive: he was physically in complete charge of himself and yet managed to turn everything upside down, using a totally different form of energy, one which cannot be found anywhere else in life other than through art, through his entire attitude to living, to the point where he was almost able to overcome his physical handicaps.

His presence on film is an outstanding example when it comes to understanding how the popular can find its way into the most refined, the most sublime art and create a combination which is even more interesting than purely formalist art of which, in the end, I am the number-one supporter, but which, without this underpinning, ends up being, I couldn't say whether better or worse, but at any rate a lot more boring.

And here I should add that, curiously, it was at the moment of seriously including the artistic element in the frame that I realised that all the pleasure, all the emotional impulses, became intensified during the process of creation; the stronger the formal commitment to a project, the more fun everything became. It surprises me that normal artists haven't understood this and that they get bored even as they seek success. This turning-upside-down of values, this living back to front, not only prolonged the fun, because it fixed it in an image; but also the reverberations it caused in real life were very much in evidence and had a much more devastating effect, which lasted a great deal longer – you just didn't want to go back to real life – than the effect created at great effort in those endless *tertúlies*; the latter required a lot more effort, and the pleasure they gave was hard to preserve. On the other hand, in a magical way, one's own production of art made it possible for this pleasure to be sustained in a more persistent and natural manner. It was a great discovery. And it had absolutely nothing to do with the result of the films, or with success, or with anything else. Nobody involved, when you make a film of this type using these principles, thinks about success or about how it's going to end up. Even with the latest film, which was listed as a competitor in Cannes, right until the last moment of the editing, which was extraordinarily difficult and hard, nobody thought for so much as a second about how the film would end up, if people would like it or not, or if it would be taken on by an important film festival. Obviously there was a kind of latent pressure — caused by the deadlines — but nobody stopped for one second to think about that. On the contrary, there was a natural expansion of playfulness and the pleasure derived from it, which justified all that paraphernalia, all that chaos, which over time and over the years I've even sometimes violently provoked, because chaos is the practical implementation of the playful. Playfulness, by its very nature, is a *festa*; think of Carnival: any form of *festa* is uncontrollable by definition, and the only way to put it into practice and manage it in an organised way is by using that ever-so-paradoxical tool which is the creation of chaos. This too became something that is at the heart of the production of all my films, with the small addition that has provided the finishing touch: something even more exciting, namely, the concept of fiction.

In a strange way, the concept of fiction, that's to say, living your life as if it were a novel, as if it were something unreal, which is nothing to do with you — you are living it but you aren't sure exactly how . . . In fiction there is no difference between daytime and night-time life; wakefulness, dream, repetitive work, the intimacy of bodies, everything is mixed up together. The specifically artistic element, as I'm sure you understand, and which came about in a natural way, was fiction. I knew how much energy it demands and I wanted to embrace it completely. On top of which, I always bore in mind Proust's commentary in *La Recherche*, when he compares the Swann character with Balzac, and says, I'm paraphrasing from memory, something like this (the narrator's speaking): 'And that day I realised that that man with such refined manners (Swann), who understood so much about art and so many other things, that man who would have killed himself rather than utter the vulgar turns of phrase and expressions to be found in their hundreds in Balzac's letters, that same man was incapable of writing *Le Curé de Tours*'* – which as you know is one of Balzac's less important novellas. When I read that sentence for the first time, it burnt itself into my mind, there hasn't been a single week when I haven't thought about it, and it gave me the necessary strength of character to come face to face with fiction, which has many nemeses, one of the most important being the fear of ridicule.

As you know, cinema is a highly tautological practice as far as reality is concerned. That is to say, if I put a camera here and film all of you, that immediately becomes a film. And all of you, because you're human beings, become actors because a camera is filming you and afterwards, when we look at it, you will be characters in a film; nothing has

---

*   'Les lettres de Balzac, par exemple, ne sont-elles pas semées de termes vulgaires que Swann eût souffert mille morts d'employer? Et cependant il est probable que Swann, si fin, si purgé de tout ridicule haïssable, eût été incapable d'écrire *La Cousine Bette* et *Le Curé de Tours*.' Marcel Proust, *Le Temps retrouvé* (Paris: Folio Classique, 1989).

changed, you are yourselves, but simply because a camera has been put here, this has become a form of fiction. In theory. Evidently, if this is done in a more complex way, the result will be a concrete sensation of fiction in a film: the mechanism which makes you think that it is real life which will go into the fiction. We have these elements, which are real people, and this, these elements, will go into the fiction, surely? And so we'll shoot it and the result will be a two-dimensional image, it isn't real life, it isn't people, but a series of two-dimensional images, and that is fiction. And this is normally the way most people think films are produced. But there is another procedure, a more sophisticated one, which is when fiction, that is to say, what there is on the screen, comes off the screen and penetrates life. This is a reverse movement which, through practice, I came to understand is produced in two different ways. Clearly, by creating a playfulness which is different to that of everyday life, being much stranger, more subversive when it comes down to it, made up of elements which are unacceptable to normality, due to their extravagant behaviour or their immorality, and that can only be done inside the bubble of a film shoot, out of which it can later little by little emerge and penetrate the rest of life; and at the same time, the second way, by creating a parallel world which is that of pure fiction, which, over the years, you realise ends up becoming a depiction of life, and not just a depiction but a procreation of the only reality which doesn't disappear: everything else ends, everything disappears, but this, on the other hand, remains. In some very fortuitous ways, as has always happened to me throughout my life, I created a mythology around this. *We* created . . . all the people who took part.

I will leave that first amateur attempt to one side; I consider an amateur film to be a *festa*, in the film there are
several *festes*, in fact almost the whole film, all the time,
everybody is having a *festa*. All the variations of the word
'festa' are in the film. It was made here with the inestimable collaboration of Josep Cortada and with the help of
Jordi Xargay who, if I'm not mistaken, was the president
of the regional council. We organised a whole popular
festa in the village of Orfes, and people said: 'Well, that's
real enough, isn't it? Did you go there to film the *festa*?'
And I answered: 'No, no . . . It was created especially,
from scratch.' And that is the embryo of what happens
when fiction enters life. And that *festa* is the only *festa*
which will stay in people's minds. The other ones pass
by, just as any worn-out daily routine passes by and, in
the end, after a few years, the same *festes* are worn out in
one's memory, unless there was some memorable image
or text or unforgettable moment. But leaving that film to
one side, we need to go to *Honor de cavalleria*, in which
Don Quixote and Sancho (it is, literally, an adaptation of
Cervantes's *Don Quixote*) end up making friends with each
other; you've all read the book or know what it's about –
well, one of the themes of the book is the birth, the slow
forging of this friendship. The film put even more stress
on this aspect of the friendship between the two characters, even a carnal friendship, one which is very tender
and loving, because my formal choice was a decision to
represent the *between-chapters*, meaning everything which
wasn't written in the book, which is what there is when
you finish one chapter and start another; in the film this
was portrayed profusely, with an affectionate physicality;
and this little fraternity between the two characters, this

poetic — and deep-rooted — friendship went on replicating and extending itself and ended up being the theme of the film.

That theme was born out of fiction. In fact Senyor Lluís Carbó had a slight acquaintance with the father of the other actor, Lluís Serrat Sr, who is also here, with his son, who later appeared in all my films; he knew him from the Banyoles lake, from when Lluís Serrat Sr worked for the municipal brigade responsible for the lake's surroundings, I think; but Lluís Carbó and Lluís Serrat's son had also come across each other; they might have seen each other when the son was little. And maybe it was for that reason, which would have helped, that they began to develop a friendship, a strange fictitious friendship, because in its early, pure stage, it began when the cameras started rolling, that is to say, when you're not yourself but are behaving like another person who is not you, in this case Don Quixote and Sancho; and at the same time this friendship developed into something real (which was a surprising thing, given the immense age difference). The gestation, the foundational moment of this friendship was recorded in this film. Obviously, I lived through this at close quarters, and everybody who worked on the film has seen, from then onwards, the consequences of that moment, of that complex iceberg of human emotion; some people will prefer the visible part, the poetry of the art in the images from the film, and others will prefer the invisible part, the humanism and human pain, each person can make their choice; but let us say that this part, the original part, was born as fiction in a way which was as fraternal as it was natural, that is to say, it formed part of the emotional relationships mentioned at the beginning of this talk and which are only possible in places like this Banyoles.

Curiously, just the other day I was in Madrid with a Spanish playwright called Fernando Arrabal; a few years before he had seen and presented *Honor de cavalleria* and this year I ran across him in Cannes, quite by chance, because he was presenting a restored version of his first film (in Cannes, there is a section called 'Cannes Classics', where they screen restorations of historically important films); I ran across him by chance, on the street, and we chatted for quite a while; and I ran into him on yet another day, also by chance, and as he is ninety years old I accompanied him to his hotel, chatting away, and I gave him my hand because he's old, and there was an uphill climb and he was getting tired, and we went on walking and chatting . . . And then a girl who was accompanying him, from the French Society of Authors, took a photo of this moment and I suppose that she put it on social media and the photo became half-famous . . . And oddly enough, the day before yesterday, after I had presented his film *Viva la muerte* in the Filmoteca Española, just as he had presented my own film a few years earlier, we started chatting. 'The hand,' he said, 'the photo of the hand is like in your film, when Don Quixote gives his hand to Sancho, twice, in the water and in the mountains,' he said, 'it's the same way of giving a hand,' he told me. And he insisted: 'Haven't you noticed, it's the same way.' And I said, 'Fuck, maybe it is.' I'd seen the photo but I hadn't paid much attention to it. 'It's the same way,' he repeated. Then I don't know what else he said, but he finished with, 'It's as if,' he said, 'it's as if . . . You know they were gay, don't you? You know that, don't you? Don Quixote and Sancho.' In fact he had written a biographical book about Cervantes called *Un esclavo llamado Cervantes* ('A Slave Called Cervantes'), and he told me that to write it he'd done some research into Cervantes's sexuality, and that when he'd been enslaved in Africa he had started with certain sexual practices which were 'against nature', and I don't know what else, and that, in the end, he was homosexual – 'Now you know.' But of course he was talking about Cervantes and everything was getting confused: Cervantes, the author, was homosexual, and Don Quixote and Sancho, the characters in the book, were also homosexual, according to him, and that 'If you and I were to give each other a hand, just like the two fictitious characters in your film who give each other a hand in the same way, which implies homosexuality, and it turns out that they were indeed giving each other a hand in that particular way, but they obviously didn't know if a similar description of that act appears in the original book of *Don Quixote*, that probably the original Don Quixote and Sancho were never based on any real people, and that if you and I were to give each other a hand in the same way, we'd be homosexual . . .' So I ended up in a spiral of confusion when he told me all this, and I thought: 'What chaos!' And 'What is he talking to me about?' But what stayed with me was a very simple idea about how reality is fabricated, which Arrabal saw very clearly, and obviously he doesn't know much, if anything, about my films, and about how this friendship had begun he knew nothing at all, and neither did I tell him about it because it was too long to explain, but he sensed that this friendship between the Don Quixote character and Sancho (Lluís Carbó and Lluís Serrat) was born of fiction and would go on developing itself in fiction . . . but also in reality.

But what's really funny is that the essential element of the relationship, as stated by Arrabal in the book itself, and in his biography of the author, and in an image from the film, is that they 'were homosexual', and it's clear that there's a little fraternity in the film, but it was later, when we shot several other films, that this friendship grew, to put it mildly, because both of them appear in all those films. In the last one, the most extraordinary one, and the one I love the most, *Singularity*, which sadly hasn't been seen very often because it was made for the Venice Biennale in the form of an installation, in this last film, which is thirteen hours long and has lots of dialogue, the two characters, oddly enough, end up becoming a common law couple. Already, in another film, *El Senyor ha fet en mi meravelles* (*The Lord Worked Wonders in Me*, 2011), which was filmed at a time when there was a debate about the legalisation of homosexual marriage, or perhaps it had already been legalised, one character asks the other, in the last scene, to marry him. Lluís Carbó's character asks Lluís Serrat's character to marry him and the film ends like that, with him telling him that he loves him very much and that he'd like to marry him. Afterwards, as I said, in the other film, *Singularity*, which was filmed years later, they are not only married but they're right there in bed, living together and they've even adopted a child. In other words, they're already married. And in fact we've seen several things related to that in the film: there's the wedding celebration, where they raise a toast with all their friends, and then there they are at work in bed, it looks as if one of them is a miner who has a mine and who also runs a brothel, because he thinks it could be a good complementary business where the workers in the mine could go and relax, and that way, he says, he would have everything under control. It turns out that this brothel doesn't work very well because all the male characters are gay and all the prostitutes are lesbians. So the business doesn't really take off. And well, this goes on fictitiously until they end up adopting a child and making plans for this child. In one of the most memorable scenes, in which the already married couple, the fruit of a friendship which had to be born and in fact was born in fiction – and also had to conclude in fiction, at the moment when they're there arguing whether to send their son to Oxford or Cambridge (the other character, played by Lluís Carbó, is an economist who advises the Bank of Ireland). And that concluded this friendship in both fiction and real life, because this was just a few months before Lluís Carbó – who was already very ill, he had cancer and was already very weak – died; he couldn't do anything else and this was, so to speak, his testament, which concluded that fiction and that human relationship which, as Arrabal said, floated, ethereal and poetic, around the question of whether they were gay or not, if 'They give each other a hand in the same way as you and I' . . . and I don't know what else . . . And they ended up celebrating the ceremony of confusion and propagating chaos, which, as I said before, is the only way in which it is possible to enter pragmatically – and programmatically – into the playfulness of life.

This had another type of resonance, aside from the one that was in the fiction, and which made it all more exciting; this other resonance deserves a chapter to itself, and not a speech to itself, because out of those initial *tertúlies* and via the interposition of fiction, it came to life, partly thanks to the international critical success of the films (this might not have been a key factor, but it made everything more extreme), with a resonance that was so strong it was almost never interrupted from then on. There were countless trips and shoots which this couple, Lluís Carbó and Lluís Serrat, always went on together, in fact, they always slept in the same room, with certain scenes that were so incredibly preposterous that, I'm telling you, they deserve not just a chapter but a whole book, or several books, just to include the unusual, insane dialogues, which are not, however, relevant here. I insist, so that it is absolutely clear, that after that seminal film, the playful element expanded in a completely insane and extraordinary way; there are witnesses to this, and for the people who lived through it, just the two trips to Mar de Plata, for example, in the south of Argentina, were so crazy that you can't even imagine it – if you didn't see it with your own eyes, you can't know what it was like.

Later on, life gave me a chance to find an external example which had made the same reverse journey, from a birth in fiction to a spreading-out in life itself, when I had the privilege of making a film with Jean-Pierre Léaud, a wonderful and unforgettable person who lived, when I met him, had lived, and still lives in a real life which contains all the elements and all the fictional structures which had made it what it was: his performances, in the beginning, in Truffaut's films and later in those of many other serious filmmakers. I have met him many times and I can assure you that we never shared the same time or space. It was thrilling to be with him for that reason, he only existed in a fictional life which made everything else disappear; and it was comforting to find that we weren't alone. We had taken the same journey, or a very similar one, me in Banyoles and he in Paris.

How can I finish this speech? Maybe it's time to wind it up. This fiction has also infiltrated real life here today, through that impulse of emotional reactions which are typical of villages; perhaps it has also infiltrated this speech, just as it keeps on infiltrating – I say this in all modesty – all the films I've made over the last few years; in *Història de la meva mort* (*Story of My Death*, 2013) five people changed their real-life partners after the end of the shoot. I think that the ambience and the spirit are identical in the later films, which have been created in the same way as the previous ones. Maybe the element of depravity has a more noticeable presence, because it is the only way to elicit a new innocence, although manipulation was also essential when it came to provoking chaos in people. But there are still certain details which are as grotesque and equally improbable now as those that came before. In fact the grotesque element is very important because the excess of this resonance of fiction in real life, through the use of playfulness, can adopt a register which is close to insanity, even coming very close to being grotesque. But risks need to be taken, one cannot be afraid. Obviously, there is an exposed, sensitive frontier, because sometimes the grotesque can simply be vulgar . . . and that is indeed

a serious risk, but it has to be taken on board and accepted. And, in this sense, the example of Lluís Carbó was
inestimable, beautiful.

I'll tell you an anecdote in which the frontier of the grotesque was almost crossed. I'll allow myself to make a sug-
gestion to the mayor because, as you will see, it is a not
unimportant one. One day, bright and early in the morning,
Lluís Carbó was at the lake, at the Mirallac hotel, I think;
I'm not sure if he was under the influence of a drink which
wasn't water. And he went off to the Tennis Club, as was his
wont. As you know, the Banyoles Tennis Club has a back
entrance, with some small steps and a ramp at the side for
bicycles and motorbikes. You can go down the ramp or you
can go down the stairs beside it. It's a bore to take the stairs
and usually everybody, even if they're on foot, descends
by the ramp, which is safe because it's got a good, rough
surface. To those people who know the place, this anecdote
will make them laugh; for those who don't, I'll try and tell it
as best I can. The steps are to the left and are shorter, and
logically they come to an end before the ramp does. Even
further to the left there is the metal fence of the tennis court
and between it and the side of the stairway which doesn't
give onto the ramp, very close by there is a very crowded
line of cypress trees (they might be looking a little worse for
wear now, they're not so crowded together, they've been dy-
ing off in stages, but I remember that, before, if a ball went
over the fence it often didn't reach the ground because the
foliage was so thick that the ball stayed in it, trapped, and
you couldn't get it back because it was so thick). They put
these cypresses next to the court to look nice and so that
people coming in wouldn't distract the players, I suppose.

Between the fence and the cypresses, on the side which is outside the court, there is a fairly narrow space. One day Lluís Carbó was going down the ramp – this was told to me by Josep Oller, a great witness – he deserves a tribute – to all these anecdotes; he has seen plenty which even I don't know about, and as he has already written several books about people who are also noteworthy, he should try and write all this material down – because as far as I know he did write down a few of these anecdotes – and make an entire book out of Lluís Carbó's exclusively grotesque anecdotes, because it would be a very funny book indeed. He, Carbó, was making his way down the ramp – which we know thanks to the totally disastrous scene which then followed and thanks to what he himself confusedly explained afterwards – and he was leaning over too much to one side, he lost his balance and tilted over to the left; seeing that he was going to fall, he tried to give himself some support with the penultimate step of the stairway, but as he wasn't able to get his balance he went shooting down the ramp, and the fact that he'd tried to put his feet on the penultimate step propelled him forward even more . . . Finally he shot out and fell straight into the mass of cypresses, in such a way that half his body, his head and trunk, were on one side of the cypresses, facing the court, with his head close to the fence, and the other half of his body, his bottom and legs, sticking out behind, with the lower part of his body firmly jammed in amongst the trees. With such bad luck that he couldn't get out or move forward or backward. So he was stuck there for twenty or thirty minutes, as far as we know, and he was discovered, if I'm not mistaken, and he'll correct me if this isn't right, but as I recall he was discovered by Josep Oller. And when Josep saw him, he tried to get him out of there. And he couldn't! He tried to pull him backwards and he couldn't! Afterwards, I already said I don't know if he was the first or the second person on the scene, Josep went to get some help, and then there were two of them trying to get Lluís Carbó out of the trees without any success; and later on, I don't know if they called his son, and I don't know how, but they managed to get him out. It needed two or three people, and they broke two or three of his ribs thanks to the friction caused by the force they needed to apply to get him out; and he was seriously ill for several days after that, he had to go to the clinic. He'd been trapped in the cypresses for half an hour or an hour, or longer, I'm not sure – but for quite a while.

Obviously, this kind of anecdote can only be told when you accept the risk of being grotesque. Because you can only take playfulness and the *festa* concept further when the frontier becomes a little vague and makes it possible, for all of us together and in a fraternal spirit, for this to happen.

From here, then, I would like to ask – should such a thing be possible – the Town Council to commission a hyper-realist bronze sculpture of the cypresses, with a body jammed in the middle and a pained expression on its face, or perhaps an ironic smile, with the head and half the body emerging from one side and the rest from the other. And maybe a piece of metal fence in front of the face, to make it even more dramatic. Or if we want to be more ironic, let his smiling face look down at us from the great beyond. And I would ask this sculpture to be placed right in the centre of Banyoles. So that everyone who walks past it and looks at it may be reminded by it of the exact spirit of the local *festes*, which begin with the *festa* of St Martirià, and which ought to be an everyday spirit. It is an extremely playful and festive spirit, on which the four words from the poster that Tàpies made for the Mercè *festa* in Barcelona, should be included. I advise you to adopt it here in Banyoles as a permanent poster and not commission any others, because it is unsurpassable; in fact all the villages in Catalonia and throughout the world should do the same; the words are: *sing, know, love, serve.*

And it is a spirit of which – if I may make one final comment about Banyoles – I am especially proud: I have been to many *festes*, to many different types of *festa*, in big cities and in villages, private ones, all kinds, with famous people, unknown people, rich people, poor people, and so on. And I can assure you – in the same way as I have claimed that all the *festes* that influenced me took place in Banyoles – that I have never had such a good time, in any other city or any other village, as I have at the *festes* that have been so much fun here, and especially Carnival which we celebrate in Banyoles, despite the not particularly spectacular nature of what happens in it; but deep down, in these emotional relationships and in this subversive spirit (and I'm telling you that I've been to many carnivals in many places around the world as well as here), in Banyoles we celebrate it, I'm telling you, in a superior fashion, thanks to the spirit of the people, thanks to the type of relationship which is established between them, which reminds me a little of the type of relationship which was established when I was young, in the nightlife I also experienced here in Banyoles, and which was still very much alive until very recently. Never, when it comes to Carnival, above all, but also when it comes to Midsummer Eve, and, it goes without saying, when it comes to the *festa* of St Martirià, have I seen anything so thrilling, so much fun, so memorable, as what I've experienced here. And I do not think that this is a subjective observation; everybody who saw it would know that it were true, as Don Quixote said of the beauty of Dulcinea, if I may make such an impossible comparison.

Have a wonderful *festa* of St Martirià; may everybody have a great time, and may it be repeated for many years to come, no matter what: the show must go on.

2

In my whole life, I have known no wise people (over a broad subject matter area) who didn't read all the time: none, zero. —Charlie Munger

It might seem strange, but the Laie bookshop in Barcelona is the physical space (along with the Banyoles Tennis Club) which has had the strongest influence on my life, as regards its personal and creative aspects. So for me it is an honour to be able to take part in the celebration of its forty years of existence. I wish it a long life and hope that it will influence many other people, as it has me.

It's my favourite bookshop in Barcelona, and I still come here with the same hopeful anticipation that I had at the start, when I was eighteen years old. It's true that sometimes I'm unfaithful . . . but that isn't so strange either, as I have never been able to walk into a bookshop and leave without having bought something. From time to time I go to the Central bookshop on Mallorca Street and Girona's Llibreria 22, both of which I also like a great deal, but nowhere am I as happy as at the Laie, maybe because I was only happy at the Blanch bookshop in Banyoles when I was a teenager. I've been an Amazon customer since the year 2000 (I was probably one of their first Spanish customers), when I bought a book by Benjamin Ivry on Rimbaud, but I never buy anything there that they have in the bookshops in Barcelona. I always travel with a Kindle, but everything that I have in digital format I also buy on paper; if only everybody was like me . . .

I've been asked to talk about cinema, but I have almost nothing to say about it. Most of the books which have influenced me are not available in a Spanish translation, and some of them are difficult to find: Jacques Lourcelles, Robin Wood, Godard, Truffaut, Paul Vecchiali, Michel Mourlet, Manny Farber, Luc Moullet, Amos Vogel . . . I didn't buy them at the Laie. In fact, I can say that these authors and critics have without a doubt influenced me a great deal more as a director than the directors themselves and the films that I've seen: what an immense power books have! My favourite is a book by Amos Vogel, *Film as a Subversive Art* – I plugged a new edition in French and wrote the prologue to it; it sold very well and the publisher is very pleased with it.

I have had no mentors and have never learnt anything from anybody. I have done everything through paper, all my idealism comes from there, from the historical avant-gardes of the early twentieth century, from *Don Quixote*, from Seneca, from the failure Stendhal . . . Everything I've earnt has been spent on books (and music): a small fortune for someone without much money. And I'll spend even more if I feel all right and can keep going: I want to give everything back to the publishing industry that it's given to me. I can't help myself, I like writers, publishers, booksellers . . . Like John Waters, I also think that being rich means you can go into a bookshop and buy whatever you feel like, without thinking about the price. Let's not forget that he's the author of the unforgettable phrase: 'We need to make books cool again. If you go home with somebody and they don't have books, don't fuck them.' By the way, I prefer his books to his films.

And for many years Karl Lagerfeld has been an idol of mine. I worship him; sadly, he died earlier this year. He always said that together with a book you should be able to buy the time to read it and, unfortunately, I have done enough things as an artist to find out that he was right. It is true that there is no better decoration in a house than shelves full of books: they give off a warmth and make us appear more intelligent than we really are to our visitors. And if people followed John Waters's reasoning we could still get something else out of them . . .

I'm happy that we're celebrating this birthday in the year that they've given the Nobel Prize to Peter Handke, another of my idols, many of whose books I did indeed buy at the Laie. Nowadays, perhaps, he doesn't sell so many books, there's nothing anyone can do about that, the world has changed – but he hasn't. I hope that the Laie never changes, either; nor the people who work here, it goes without saying. They're fine just as they are. Happy birthday.

A text written on the occasion of the fortieth anniversary of the Laie bookshop in Barcelona, 2020.

3

Films are about personality: the better the personality, the
better the film. —Paul Morrissey

The recuperation of the actor as a *performer*, as the gener-
ator of fatal, unrepeatable gestures, as a creator of a fate
which is at the same time both human and plastic, has
been my obsession ever since I started to work in cinema.
Manny Farber, like Warhol and Paul Morrissey, traced the
decadence of the actor back to the 1950s. He longed for
the films of the 1930s, in which the actor's gaze was even
more important than their hairdo (a 'balustrade'), their
gestures more important than their significance. All the
stylisation of a film was in the service of the actor and not
the other way round (the lighting wasn't an abstract thing
which was the fruit of the imagination of the director of
photography, it highlighted the expression of the actors!).
Hence the terrible commentary of Paulette Goddard on the
decadence of Chaplin: 'Max Eastman and Upton Sinclair
destroyed Charlie by treating everything he did as intellectual; afterwards he didn't know anymore how to do what
he did.' Paulette, Chaplin's wife, portrayed him as a frus-
trated writer who, given his uselessness when it came to
written language, decided to make literature with images.
The presence of the actor was lost ('before, his films
were all movement, movement and mime') and meaning
appeared. Hence the predilection of all avant-garde art for

the mechanical purity of Keaton, for the wild and savage
purity of Harry Langdon, or in the case of Manny Farber,
for Laurel and Hardy: their staging was, according to him,
'dispersed', and instead of being virtuosos at deploying
space – like Chaplin – they 'dissolved' it around them;
Laurel and Hardy are lost in their own frame, and in a dis-
turbing way, they do not know how to use it 'aesthetically
or egoistically' to their own benefit.[*]

All the advances related to staging in film history have had
a narrative purpose. I have always considered it absurd
to think about staging, and I have avoided believing that
it could have any relevance to the aesthetic quality of the
film. I have shot in digital, because it was simpler when
it came to *serving* the actors, and my whole methodology
boils down to the principle that technique should always
be prepared to capture the actor's inspiration, and that
this can happen in the most unforeseen moments or circumstances. Whatever form this wait might take, it pro-
duces a *tension*, and out of something as simple as this,
the most refined staging can emerge, because it is latent.
Rather, to make the actor wait is to turn him into an 'ac-
cessory', into an 'ambulant receptacle of the production
team'; as in theatre, the actor is frequently nothing but
a receptacle of the word. The actor is not a 'spot' in the
image, nor another shape, he is the emotion that derives
from a dramaturgy: the dramaturgy of his presence. The
moving image is not fetishistic; it is moral, substantial,
because of time, an element that only the actor can make
visible for us. Each of his gestures has an effect, it does so

[*]   Manny Farber, *Negative Space: Manny Farber on the Movies* (New York:
        Da Capo Press, 1998), 370.

just when the gesture is taking place, and only the face of the actor can garner it.

All films should only come to life on the screen. Nothing of what we see should have happened before in reality. Only the camera should be able to record what is essential to the actor; people working on the shoot should not be able to perceive it. This is why, increasingly, I have got used to not observing what is happening on set while shooting. Each scene should be new, with new dialogues, new turning points, and, if it has already been watched, it becomes old and wasted. It cannot even be thought of, nor conceived in a physical sense. The scene only exists in the face of the actor, and his spontaneous reaction is what we gaze at as spectators. What is the difference in our mind between a 'magical' Saturday night party and a boring one? They are not comparable. Nevertheless, they involve the same people, the same space, the same action. In plastic terms, they are very similar. But the difference in intensity with regard to the effect that they exert on us is unquestionable. Only the camera can capture this difference without interpreting it.

As Manny Farber says, the actor cannot be 'alive' as a character and maintain the style of the film at the same time. He himself is the style. He creates a symbiosis with set, rhythm, colour. But he offers no meanings. What does a gesture mean? A gaze? Nothing. Gerardo Diego once read one of his Creationist poems aloud; someone asked him what he meant to say with those verses, and he answered: 'I meant what I said, because if I'd meant to say something else, I would have said it.' An actor's gestures, his gaze, provide their own meaning. The great actor does not represent, nor even express; he simply is. Perhaps his gestures work as an epiphany of the kinetic life, of the emphatic gesture and the poetic spoken word: they offer, as a presence and as a gift, something which is beyond reality, as the poet Pere Gimferrer put it. But nothing more. Only great actors, like great poems, can stand the weight of being signifiers without falling to pieces. Only great directors (Bene, Warhol, Straub) have the discipline to repress their own indiscretion, and to accept each actor as a form of celebration.

The most embarrassing effect of not accepting the dramaturgy of presence as the essential aim — the immanency — of every actor, and instead, of looking for the confirmation of their existence by means of the effects that they create, is the emergence of 'psychology', and what is even worse, the fact that this psychology is quantifiable: tears are shed, just as is sweat, saliva, semen . . . The greater the quantity of material, mathematically, the greater the veracity and, therefore, the greater the profitability (a tangible good is given to the viewer in return for their money). The actor becomes the character in a quantifiable way and, therefore, controllable. Or, what is more or less the same thing from an emotional point of view: the presence of the actor is better appreciated when confronted with his own absence (staging). And besides, as Barthes pointed out, this 'actor's combustion' is adorned with spiritualistic justifications: the actor gives himself over to the demon of representation, 'he sacrifices himself, allows himself to be eaten up from inside by his role: his generosity, the gift of his body to Art, his physical labour are worthy of pity and admiration'.* The evidence of his labour is irrefutable. And it turns into style: style is a bourgeois evasion when faced with the deep mystery of a pure presence in *Nostra Signora dei Turchi* (Carmelo Bene, 1968).

Manny Farber despises the kind of interpretation done by Jeanne Moreau in *Jules et Jim* (François Truffaut, 1961) and *The Trial* (Orson Welles, 1962), but in 1966 he had not yet seen an even more unfortunate performance: her presence in *Une Histoire immortelle* (Orson Welles, 1968) is so untranscendental, that her figure seems to be painted onto badly-pasted wallpaper. Because the core of every cinematographic performance, according to Farber, is the suggestive material that hovers at the edges of each role, and never its psychological-ontological centre: 'Quirks of physiognomy, private thoughts of the actor about himself, misalliances where the body isn't delineating the role, but is running on a tangent to it.'† Also, in the progressive re-finement of my methodology, and only through practical experience, without bearing in mind any theoretical read-ings, I discarded the possibility that the centre of a role, that is to say, the deep projection of a character, could have any aesthetic validity. ('I'm only interested in the air above the actor's head, never in what's inside it, and therefore it's useless to stare at what is happening while shooting,' I once declared). Honestly, and I think this is the basis of my infallible method for directing actors, I consider it a sac-rilege for me to gaze at a pure performance at the risk of

*   Roland Barthes, *Mythologies*, translated by Richard Howard and
     Annette Lavers (New York City: Hill and Wang, 2012), 120.
†   Manny Farber, 'Cartooned Hip Acting', in Robert Polito, ed., *Farber on
     Film: The Complete Film Writings of Manny Farber* (New York: Library
     Of America, 2009), 588.

spoiling it. I trust that the camera will capture their most far-reaching profiles; and, above all, due to my Olympian contempt for cinema as an art form, what I am doing does not interest me at all.

First published in *Cinema Comparat/ive Cinema* 2, no. 4 (autumn 2014): 93–6.

4

How are you feeling, Albert? What have you been up to recently?
Better than ever, as usual. And because of what's brought
us here, I've dedicated myself to something that I can't
do very often for lack of time: listening to an opera and
reading the libretto at the same time. I also have to tell
you that often this isn't very edifying, because librettos
are, traditionally, banal and dull, something which, para-
doxically, makes them suitable for certain stage directors
to have their say with, while at the same time making a
detailed, complex, rich and involuntary description of
their own ignorance. Let's say they're on the same level.
But it's surprising that even the librettos of a genius like
Wagner are so silly and uninteresting: in a word, infantile.
It makes you wonder if this ridiculous basis might not be
a necessary condition for sublime music to be enjoyed at
a fully physical level, without any intellectual distortions.
In the same way, it's still curious that many dilettantes and
opera fanatics are not fans of any other artistic discipline,
so far as I can see.

Don't you know of any exceptions?
Of competent directors or of suggestive librettos? Or of
more-culturally-aware dilettantes?

The first two.

Beaumarchais's ones are a bit better than the rest, *The Marriage of Figaro* and *The Barber of Seville. Othello* and *Falstaff* are also good, and I especially like *Ariadne auf Naxos* which plays, precisely, with the above-mentioned presuppositions. It reminds me of the ambience of films like *The Band Wagon* and *The Red Shoes* and also Frank Borzage's *I've Always Loved You.* I like the world of show business, it's a way of life, in fact I decided to become a film director and artist in order to live in it permanently, something which I have without a doubt managed to do . . . And in my own way I've improved with a rather unique use of digital technology, which makes it possible for shoots to be far more anarchic and under much less pressure from technical factors. The madness and the subversive element both increase exponentially, as does the resulting fun. This is harder to find in theatre or opera, of course, although I haven't abandoned the idea of finding a way to do the same thing with them some day. Life in itself is a representation, so why not accept that fully and take all the moral consequences? That's show business. But such anarchy has to be imposed methodically, something which sounds like another paradox, as is the imposition of licentiousness by the use of force, as can be seen in my last film but one, *Liberté.* This ambivalence is at the very heart of the spectacle. It's the cruelty within it, exemplified by the saying 'The show must go on' . . . no matter how sad the circumstances. This phrase has always impressed me and I've also had to put it into practice in certain difficult situations. It's tyrannical, but it leads to the common good of those who stay the course, don't you think? It's the main theme of the three above-mentioned films.

What about those stage directors who are exceptions?
I'm sorry, but this subject bores me, it's too negative. Let's talk about something else, if you don't mind.

Does the poor quality of stage directors sicken you?
Not exactly, but I do find that this quality is disproportionate and terribly unimaginative. It has become a routine and the abandonment of the contemporary repertoire of serious writers in the programming of the larger theatres doesn't help at all. Unpublished works can also help in the search for new sensations and new ways of working, something which is more difficult with a traditional repertoire, which suffers from the pressure of cliché. Leaving to one side the aesthetic emotion generated by live music, the two best examples of opera staging ever recorded were made by two film directors, who took advantage, certainly, of certain possibilities of a controlled cinematographic mise-en-scène . . . But the result is so overwhelmingly superior that this little bit of help is irrelevant, it's more a matter of criteria and concepts.

Who are you referring to?
Straub's *Moses and Aran* and Syberberg's *Parsifal*. The musical director of the first one, by the way, was Michael Gielen. They are two visual odes to the glory of the opera. Unbeatable. It isn't worth going to see anything live if you've got that at home. It is true that there are *documents* or *captures* of some interesting moments, like Heiner Müller's *Tristan and Isolde*, but to make things clear we could say that there is more of the *musical* and the *operatic* in any clip from any film by Werner Schroeter dedicated to this subject than in any of the more pompous

and famous stagings done by the great contemporary directors.

And the level of provocation?
I like provocation, it's hygienic; but nobody today is capable of so much as enunciating a politically incorrect idea, even when they don't really believe in it. The level of falseness and cowardice in the well-paid artistic scene is ghastly. And let's not even talk about what happens when those ideas which are so difficult to bring to the table turn out to be great, obvious truths except for the people in the *extreme centre*, as Philippe Muray would put it. This battle having been lost, we can only console ourselves by thinking that the only possible provocation nowadays is to make something which is strictly serious to the bitter end, without worrying if people are going to like it, or if it will be more or less understood.

Do you miss the older forms of provocation?
Of course I do, don't you? What Donald Trump says in his tweets is funnier, more interesting and more provocative than anything that professional comics or playwrights are doing, who are very well paid, by the way, and who only know how to laugh at the weak and say things which today any three-year-old child knows. Look what happened to *Charlie Hebdo*. Effective provocation is risky and can end badly, it's an absolute to some extent, and for that reason all of it should be forgiven. And it's better when it tries to scandalise against its own best interests . . . when it's truly suicidal. Then, as if by a miracle, it can become spectral, or even revelatory, the involuntary bearer of tremendous lucidity, which is the case with Donald Trump, who being

a politician (so to speak) who has the most irresponsible ideas in the world, is unexpectedly converted into a popular politician, with more votes and better loved than his responsible rivals. But I suspect we're getting off the subject. Even though the parallel with the artistical and theatrical world strikes me as being obvious.

But that doesn't happen with authentic contemporary art. Its formal evolution is too complex to be suddenly appreciated on the basis of a misunderstanding.
That depends: sometimes it does happen; take the case of Houellebecq. Success has protected him, and his arguments have become more difficult to contend with, first because they can't simply be repressed by means of public ostracism, which is the most usual form of attack nowadays against the freedom of expression and personal commitment. And even his enemies think that if Houellebecq is successful and they aren't, there must be some reason for that . . . As you can imagine, I myself, on the other hand, have never felt the temptation to think in that way.

Is there any provocation which, according to you, precisely because it's too risky, isn't worth making?
The answer's already in the question: no. It is *precisely* the fact of its being *too* risky which gives it full meaning, among other things because it stops us from taking our freedoms a step backward, and especially that freedom which is perhaps most important: freedom of expression. The right to say stupid things or to tell lies is more important collectively than that of telling the truth or making intelligent observations (Robbe-Grillet also believed this). Fake news is a blessing. Moreover, if it's fake, how do we know it's fake news? It's in

this world that I feel fine, like a fish in water. And I'm sorry if we've strayed from the original subject, but to some extent it can be seen that I feed off strong obsessions.

Not to worry, Albert. It's been a pleasure.
Thank you for inviting me. I'm very happy that you've enjoyed it. If you liked it, that's good enough for me.

See you later.

A self-interview first published in *Obsessió* (Barcelona: Cercle del Liceu, 2020).

Afterword: Conceptual Art

Alexander García Düttmann

'One small village of indomitable Catalans still holds out against the invaders.'* This one sentence, which is almost a quotation, should suffice to make you understand that I have just reread the long tribute my friend Albert Serra paid to his native hometown and its inhabitants in October 2022, on the occasion of the local festivities of St Martirià, the patron saint of Banyoles. For just as he asks himself how the cultural and the genetic elements intersect in his becoming an artist, how the freedom of choice inscribed in his culture and the force of resolution inscribed in his character interact with each other, Serra presents Banyoles as a stronghold, as an unassailable base and a solid frame, as an anchoring place and a place of no return.

A place of no return? Yes, since Serra is unable not to return constantly to Banyoles. He cannot and does not wish to leave it behind. No matter where he goes, it is from Banyoles that he sets about his business. Everything begins there and exceeds the arbitrary connotations of birth. Banyoles is more than a physical space. It is, as Serra puts it, a 'concept', something mental in the double sense of the

---

* As is well known, every adventure of Asterix the Gaul begins with the following legend: 'The year is 50 BC. Gaul is entirely occupied by the Romans. Well, not entirely! One small village of indomitable Gauls still holds out against the invaders.'

expression, an enabling limitation, an empowering fixation or even a vivifying paralysis and a life-affirming and spirited martyrdom that the filmmaker cannot renounce without risking a break so radical that it would threaten his artistry. Banyoles as a 'concept', as an immemorial and hence inextricable mixture of the cultural and the genetic, proves indomitable. It turns its true inhabitants – not necessarily the property owners who come up from Barcelona – into indomitable people who resist integration and, by way not of a declared intention but of their very existence, insist on their peculiarity. Have they sprung up from the lake that is one of Banyoles's most popular sights?

The peculiarity manifests itself preferably at night and in a playful aspect, in the gatherings known as *tertúlies*, in the infinite, once erudite and today casual conversations that begin in the afternoon and, at least in Banyoles, extend into the wee hours and beyond. Does it also manifest itself in the scene of painful slapstick that may ensue when one of the locals leaves the Tennis Club through a small backdoor and trips down a ramp? From the outside, it is impossible to break through the resourceful, innocent, intimate, trusting, disrespectful, impulsive, driven, vulnerable and shared wackiness, drollness and freakishness that Serra celebrates and that he tries to emulate on his sets, as if they carried the 'concept' of Banyoles to any conceivable location in the world, from a wood in the south-east of Portugal to a landscape in Iceland or a beach in the vicinity of Pape'etē in French Polynesia. Banyoles is a universal and at the same time impenetrable 'concept', a kind of absolute *concetto* that brings together two incomparable and incompatible dimensions – or rather, a dimension and a point, an opening and a closure. The frame holds tight. Sometimes, however, the latent subversive and libidinous forces it encloses may require a rupture that fissures the frame. Serra is a cautious man. When the frame cracks because of the pressure generated within it, an escape occurs. Yet the centrifugal force must not create havoc. It must allow itself to be channelled and steered in a certain direction, so that its effects are not too destructive. Banyoles is a demanding 'concept'. It must be if fun is to be had chatting with friends in a bar, or with acquaintances close and vague in a social club. It must be if fun is to be had making a film on familiar or remote grounds, collectively and under the director's eye, which comes into its own in the editing room.

A *tertúlia* and a film start out conventionally and become all the more unpredictable as the conversation unravels and the end of the shoot approaches. Contrary to what common sense suggests, chaos, the chaos on which an achievement depends, the emergence of a form, is never to be found in the beginning but always arises in the final phase, at least in the course of a creative undertaking. Serra provides a precise definition of chaos. It is supposed to be a practical execution of playfulness and hence something created rather than something given. How, exactly, does chaos relate to art and artwork, chaos as something created that comes to the fore when a long and free-flowing conversation goes wild, when, after a game of tennis, a misstep happens, or when the last stages of a shoot are reached? Is chaos a blending of fiction and reality that does not permit disambiguation and that takes shape in an artwork, or in certain moments to be found in an artwork?

When fiction acquires a reality of its own, it transforms, say, a handshake into a memorable and emblematic handshake that keeps persevering in its singularity. Here, playfulness – pretending one shakes hands in the presence of a camera – turns into chaos. Serra pushes the acting bodies to a limit where they no longer shake hands knowingly, or barely so. Such chaos gives rise to form. The handshake is memorable and its traces cannot be erased. This is the case not because it is a handshake in general, the handshake of all handshakes, as it were, but because it is precisely *this* – and not *that* – handshake. Chaos gives rise to a form that leaves little room for recognition, for the application of the general concept of a handshake to a particular case. However, this does not mean that the handshake vanishes into the ineffable. Does the 'concept' of Banyoles transform Serra into a Kantian, that is into an advocate of beauty, pleasurable lingering, an intensification of life? Perhaps. Serra's filmic images tend to be sensuous, painterly, lavish. Seldom are they trashy.

Yet there seems to be an important difference. Serra radicalises the argument by replacing the particular, on which the Kantian conception is based, with the singular. In Kant, the particular elicits a subjective judgement expressive of a pleasure that is not just mine and that speaks as if with a universal voice: 'This is beautiful.' When it does so, it cancels out cognitive judgements of the type: 'This is beautiful in itself,' or 'This is a beautiful object.' It intimates a purposefulness without a purpose, a purposefulness that can only be felt. Only cognitive judgements apply concepts to objects, indicate a purpose and not merely a purposefulness. The particular to which the subjective judgement refers resembles the singular, is actually the singular, though somewhat entrapped. It is the singular that keeps itself at bay. In Serra, the singular retains a wackiness, a drollness and a freakishness. It ceases to intimate purposefulness.

Conversely, the universal ceases to be the one traditionally attributed to truth, and resembles much more an opening and a dimension that expand between the earth and the skies. The concept of Banyoles denotes both, the opaqueness inherent in this opening and this dimension, and the lucidity that they bestow upon the opaque. The relation or non-relation between the singular and the universal, between the point and the dimension, harbours chaos. Serra's concern with − or commitment to − form, of which he speaks in his toast to Banyoles, to the 'concept' of Banyoles, seeks, in the recreation of the small town on a set, or in the reinvention of its concept as a set, a form injected with uncertainty. It is the uncertainty of exhaustion and dissemination. It is the uncertainty of a heightening and a diminishing that affect conversation when it liberates itself from a temporal framework and filming when it keeps coming to an end.

What happens when fiction, as it acquires a reality of its own, irradiates into reality? If, once again, one sticks to one of the examples Serra gives − the example of a companionship between two actors that, in fiction, turns into male homosexual love and then crosses the border between reality and fiction once more, now in the opposite direction, back to reality, so to speak − what appears to happen is that it no longer matters whether the two actors, the two characters they play, sleep with each other, or not, suck each other's cocks, or not, penetrate each other, or not. They do because they no longer do. They have entered a strange zone of indistinction, in which they are neither chained to gravity – to sexuality – nor elevated to the clunky ideality of make-believe. Occasionally, it is this zone that I think I may have entered with Albert Serra. The event could not have taken place without the 'concept' of Banyoles. This is the lesson of his tribute or toast.

While Banyoles means little to me, its 'concept' is a precious gift. Sadly, my metropolitan impatience, or my envy, does not value it enough. Joyfully, though, I have been to Banyoles. Its 'concept' has disclosed itself to me, without having had to take a bus.